WRITING SENTENCES WORKBOOK

How to Write Sentences People Love to Read!

WRITING SENTENCES WORKBOOK

How to Write Sentences People Love to Read!

HERON BOOKS

Published by
Heron Books, Inc.
20950 SW Rock Creek Road
Sheridan, OR 97378

heronbooks.com

First Edition © 2021, 2025 Heron Books
All Rights Reserved

ISBN: 978-0-89739-145-0

Printed in the USA

11 September 2025

In This Book

This book belongs to:

Activity 1
Crossword Puzzle

Fill in this crossword puzzle with nouns that name the things shown on the next page.

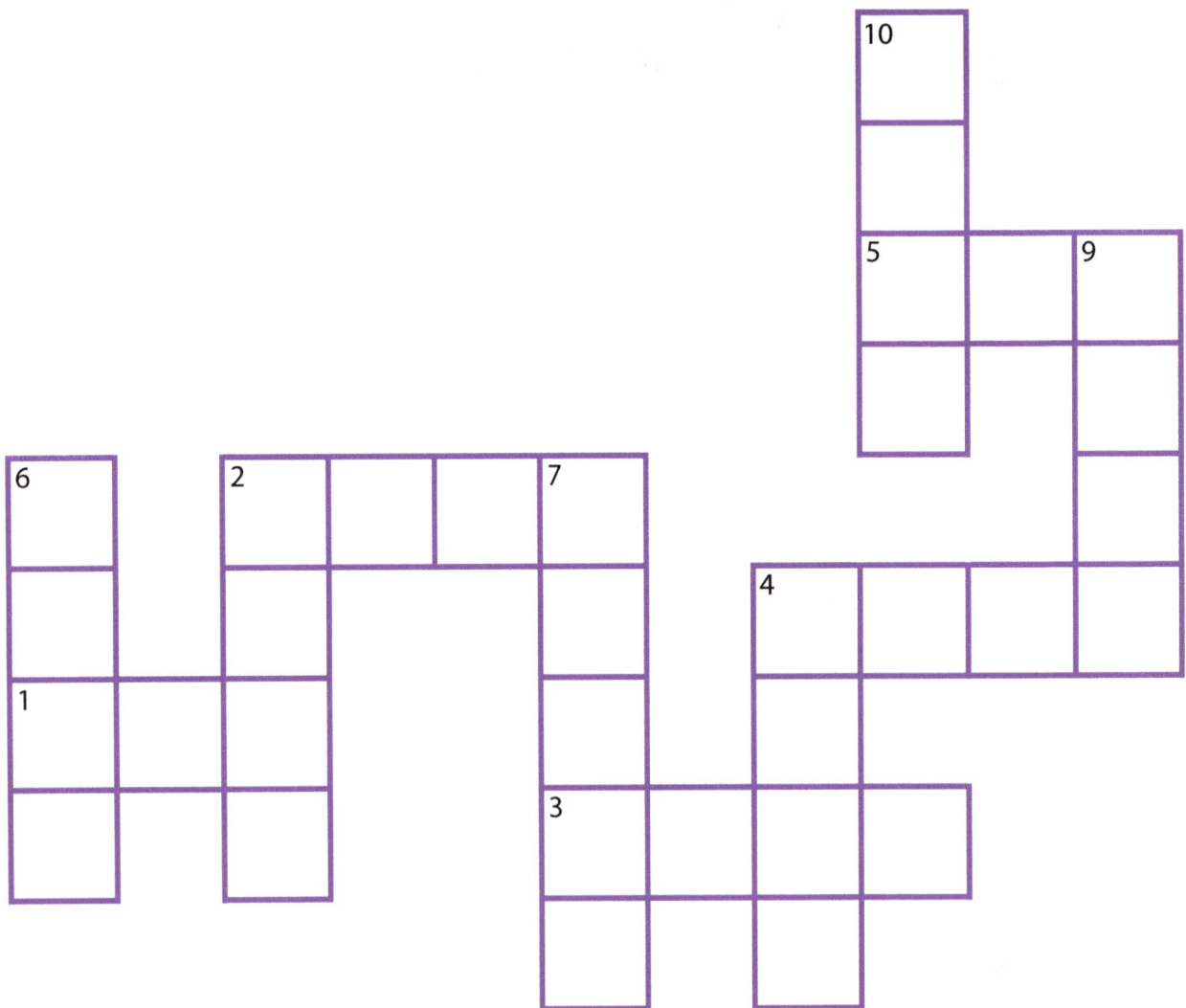

Across

1.

2.

3.

4.

5.

Down

2.

4.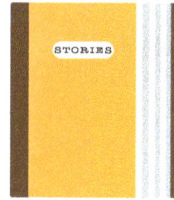

6.

7.

9.

10.

Activity 2
Find the Nouns

Draw a line under each noun in these sentences.

Jackson talked to Roy.

Jorge saw the bus.

The girl walked to the store.

Matthew jumped over the fence.

The cat licked its paws.

The road was covered with leaves.

The carpenter built a cabinet.

Eliza went to the park.

My friend rang the doorbell twice.

The boys walked to school together.

Activity 3
Fill in the Nouns

Fill in the blank spaces with nouns.

There's a _____ in the yard.

The _____ is green.

It is hard to pick up a _____ .

His _____ is broken.

My favorite animal is a _____ .

I saw an enormous _____ yesterday.

I like to ride in a _____ . It goes fast

along the _____ . I put my hand

out the _____ and wave

at _____ .

Activity 4
Action Verb Game

Write a sentence with one action verb.

_____

_____

Now take out the verb and write the sentence over with another action verb.

_____

_____

Change the verb over and over to make as many new sentences as you can. (You don't have to use all the lines.)

_____

_____

_____

_____

_____

_____

Activity 5
Noun and Verb Game

Using pencil, write a story of at least five sentences. Be sure to include action verbs in your story.

_____

_____

_____

_____

_____

_____

_____

_____

Now erase the nouns and action verbs from your story and leave a blank space where those words were. Write "noun" or "action verb" under each blank space.

Have another person fill in the blank spaces. Then read your story with the new words.

Activity 6
Being Verbs

Here are the most common being verbs:

be, being, is, am, are, was, were

Write a being verb in each blank space.

Juan will _____ happy.

They _____ here yesterday.

The duck _____ loud.

After dinner she _____ full.

The sleepy boy _____ grumpy.

They _____ funny.

The dog and the cat _____ friends.

The pizza in the oven _____ done.

They _____ on the grass.

Kamal _____ happy on his birthday.

Activity 7
Helping Verbs

Here are some common helping verbs:

**can, could, would, should, may, must,
might, do, does, did, will, have, has, had,
am, are, is, was, were**

Write a helping verb with an action verb in each blank space.

The elephant _____ on the mouse.

Eden _____ to the park.

They _____ on the grass.

He _____ the ball.

The duck _____ .

The dog and the cat _____ together.

Write a helping verb with a being verb in each blank space.

Juan _____ tall.

The ducks _____ loud.

After dinner he _____ full.

Kittens _____ funny.

The pizza in the oven _____ done.

Kai _____ here tomorrow.

Activity 8
Main Verbs and Helping Verbs

Draw a line under the verb or verbs in each of these sentences. If the verb is just a main verb, write main on the line after the sentence. If there is a helping verb, write <u>helping</u> on the line

The horse jumped over the fence. _____

I thought of an interesting story. _____

I am pulling the wagon. _____

That elephant lives at the zoo. _____

She is wearing her best dress. _____

He has finished his drawing. _____

Anastasia likes her little brother. _____

The horse ran fast in the race. _____

I have eaten breakfast. _____

The garden is growing well this year. _____

He acts happy. _____

We were talking loud. _____

I brought my ball to the park. _____

Activity 9
Noun or Verb?

Draw a line under each noun and a circle around each verb in these sentences. Hint: Some of the verbs have a helping verb and a main verb.

Jennifer might take the bus.

Most people like paintings.

Sean can ride horses every weekend.

My father paints beautiful pictures.

A plastic jacket covers the book.

Dara will name the baby.

Vegetables grow in Oregon.

The puppy will sleep after dinner.

Aki made a great baseball play.

Alia should write a book someday.

That bowl has a tight cover.

Activity 10
Verb Tenses

Underline the verb in each sentence. Write on the line what tense the verb is.

A caterpillar becomes a butterfly. _____

We walk to the store on the corner. _____

Tai will win the spelling bee. _____

The giraffe is very tall. _____

My mom dug a huge hole in the yard. _____

We will stay at the beach all day. _____

My dad and I cleaned the whole house! _____

Misha brought a sandwich today. _____

Jenna will swim in a race on Saturday. _____

That bell rings loudly. _____

The mouse chased the cat away! _____

I will get a big piece of cake. _____

Activity 11
Present Tense Verbs

Pick a verb from the list at the top of each column. Use your verb to complete the sentences below. Notice when you need to add *s* or *es* to make the verb sound right.

jog, skip, run, laugh, kick, dream, grow

rush, dash, march, wash, crash, push, wish

I _____ .

I _____ .

The animals _____ .

The animals _____ .

You _____ .

You _____ .

She _____ .

She _____ .

The family _____ .

The family _____ .

We _____ .

We _____ .

The boy _____ .

The boy _____ .

They _____ .

They _____ .

Activity 12
Regular or Irregular?

For these verbs, write down the past tense and tell if they are regular or irregular.

Present	Past	Regular or Irregular?
walk		
run		
sing		
climb		
throw		
sail		
pile		
sell		
know		
sit		
bring		
work		

Activity 13
Continuing Action

Change each sentence to show continuing action. Keep the same tense.

Examples:
He runs.   *He is running.*
The horse ran.   *The horse was running.*
I will run the race today.   *I will be running the race today.*

A dog barks.   A dog _____ .

The cat purred.   The cat _____ .

I pick apples.   I _____ apples.

Tia will eat the ice cream.   Tia _____ the ice cream.

My sister waits.   My sister _____ .

They laughed.   They _____ .

You sang to me.   You _____ to me.

The horse drank some water.   The horse _____ some water.

They will come to school.   They _____ .

He grows.   He _____ .

We swam every day.   We _____ every day.

She will write letters.   She _____ letters.

Activity 14
Adjectives

Decide on one noun to use for this activity. It doesn't have to make sense! Write it down after each of these adjectives and decide which one you like best with that noun. Draw a circle around that one.

beautiful _____

ugly _____

bright _____

green _____

dancing _____

tiny _____

damp _____

old _____

Activity 15
Add the Adjectives

Here is a story with no adjectives.

The dog ran up to a boy. He put out his tongue and gave the boy a lick on the hand. Then the boy threw a stick for the dog to catch. The dog ran to pick up the stick. He brought the stick back and dropped it on the ground. The boy rewarded the dog with a treat.

Kind of boring, isn't it? Your job is to make the story more interesting, using adjectives.

Fill in the blanks as many different adjectives as you can.

The _____ dog ran up to the _____ boy. He put out

his _____ tongue and gave the boy a _____

lick on his _____ hand. Then the boy threw a _____

stick for the _____ dog to catch. The dog ran to pick up the

_____ stick. He brought the stick back and dropped it on the

_____ ground. The boy rewarded the dog with a _____

treat.

Now read both stories to another person and see what they think of each one.

Activity 16
Adverbs with Verbs

For each sentence, underline the verb and circle the adverb that tells more about how, when or where the verb happens.

How:

    The cat lazily stretched in the sun.

    The dog ran excitedly to her food.

    A bird sang softly in the tree.

    Dan carefully folded his paper airplane.

When:

    We will have dinner soon.

    I already read that book.

    Can we meet later?

    Yesterday we played basketball.

Where:

    We went there last year.

    The balloon rose high in the sky.

    That baby stays close to her brother.

    He ran away from the alligator.

Activity 17
Adverbs with Adjectives

Here are some adverbs that can tell more about adjectives.

> **too, so, more, very, totally, super, really, dark, light, extremely, slightly, quite, terribly**

For each of these sentences, pick an adverb to tell more about the adjective.

That is a _____ ugly dog.

A _____ angry cat hissed at me.

I have a _____ purple marker.

This candy is _____ sweet.

I just ate a _____ good cookie!

That puzzle was _____ easy!

Her vacation was _____ fun than mine.

Min's hair got _____ wet from the rain.

Activity 18
Adverbs with Other Adverbs

Here are some adverbs that can tell more about other adverbs.

most, always, super, slightly, so, very, really, almost, much, too, terribly

For each of these sentences, pick an adverb to tell more about the other adverb.

That is the _____ nicely written note.

The storm is _____ extremely loud!

This bus is _____ really slow.

Paint the wall a _____ light brown.

That dog jumps _____ high!

My bike goes _____ faster than yours.

That cat acts _____ friendly.

The trip took _____ longer than we expected.

Activity 19
A, An or The

Use *a* or *an* to complete each sentence.

I touched _____ ostrich at the zoo.

My family is leaving on _____ vacation in _____ hour.

I wish I had _____ horse of my own.

We baked _____ apple pie yesterday.

Use a, an or the to fill in the blanks in these sentences.

_____ boy came to see _____ show.

He dropped _____ egg on _____ kitchen floor.

_____ children wanted _____ horse of their own.

_____ family wanted to go to _____ zoo

One of _____ horses got _____ apple.

Mother said we should be home in _____ hour.

_____ river is _____ good place to swim.

Activity 20
Stopping Sentences

Read each sentence, and decide if it should have a period, a question mark or an exclamation point. Then write the correct punctuation mark at the end of the sentence.

I like to go swimming

Watch out for that rock

Do you want to go

He doesn't like me

Is that his mother

Look at that elephant

I want to go to the movies

We played at my house yesterday

Wow, that flower is beautiful

Are you going to the circus today

Activity 21

Add the Commas

Put the correct punctuation in these sentences. Add commas where they are needed.

We will visit New York Washington and Baltimore.

Will we go to the circus the park or the beach?

I need pants sweaters shirts sandals and a bathing suit for camp.

There are elephants zebras camels and hippos in Africa.

Put commas in this letter.

Dear Mom

I am soooo excited about my birthday party! I have been thinking of what my friends would like to eat.

Could you please get these things for my party:

Chips dip cupcakes fruit and juice.

Thanks!

Love Carrie

Activity 22
Capital Letters

Circle the words that should start with a capital letter.

united states	table	december	friday
bill	oregon	spring	ralph
dog	ball	kathy	san francisco
tuesday	man	february	bike
insect	is	oak street	red river

Fix the Capital Letters

Copy this story on the lines below. Put capital letters in all the places where they belong.

on tuesday mike and ann went to the park with their pet dog spot. it was december and the sky was cloudy. spot had lots of fun. the next day mike and ann went to school. the name of their school was wildwood school. spot couldn't go to school. he stayed home and played with a cat named fluffy.

_____

_____

_____

_____

_____

_____

Find the Subjects

Underline the subject in each sentence.

The dog chased the cat up a tree.

Will she climb that ladder?

Olivia went to a fancy restaurant.

You won the race!

Ling took a lot of pictures at my party.

Is that your birthday cake?

Lightning flashed brightly in the sky.

That storm knocked down the tree!

The baby smiled for his sister.

The clown laughed and danced in the circus.

Can you carry this heavy bag?

The Clarks enjoyed the peaceful trip.

Activity 25
Complete or Incomplete?

Write complete in front of each sentence that is complete. Put an X in front of each group of words that is not a complete sentence.

The boy ran outside.

The pretty flowers.

The horse jumped over the fence.

Was in the house.

Baako cried.

Grows in the garden.

By the time we arrived.

The puppy yelped.

I am so surprised.

Was delicious pizza.

Activity 26
Run-on Sentences

Some of the groups of words below are run-on sentences and some are not. If it is a run-on sentence, write run-on after it.

The boy ran around the track he ran fastest. _____

The girl was so happy to have very kind friends. _____

The goats played a cat slept. _____

It was an exciting book that he read with his parents. _____

My father made very tasty pancakes and served them with syrup. _____

After she saw that movie she was too excited to sleep she went for a walk instead. _____

We have a dog and a cat they love to play games and run around. _____

Carrie has a green bike and a blue skateboard. _____

www.ingramcontent.com/pod-product-compliance
Lightning Source LLC
Chambersburg PA
CBHW081012040426
42443CB00016B/3494